# HERE BE LI~~ONS~~

by Stéphane Olr~

Translated from the ~

by Neil Bartlet~

This translation was commissioned by Theatre of Europe
in co-production with Print Room at the Coronet
where it received its UK premiere on 10 June 2015.

HERE BE LIONS was first produced in France by la Revue
Éclair and Le Château de la Roche Guyon under the
title HIC SUNT LEONES, published by Les Éditions de
l'Amandier in the series La Bibliothèque Fantôme.

Print Room at the Coronet in association with Theatre of Europe presents
d(ARE) / HERE BE LIONS
by Sandrine Buring, Stéphane Olry and la Revue Éclair,
text translated by Neil Bartlett

d(ARE) choreographed and performed by **Sandrine Buring**
*HERE BE LIONS* directed by **Stéphane Olry** and **Corine Miret**,
performed by **Hayley Carmichael** and **Phil Minton**

Lighting Designer and Technical Director **Luc Jenny**


Special Thanks to:
Yves Chevallier (Director of Château de La Roche-Guyon),
Laurent Goldring, Isabelle Duthoit, Eamonn Bedford,
Institut Français du Royaume-Uni

This project is supported by the Institut Français
as part of the Théâtre Export programme

## SANDRINE BURING
### Choreographer and Dancer

Sandrine Buring was a gymnast, footballer, barmaid, florist and veterinary assistant before establishing herself as a choreographer and dancer. She has collaborated on a number of productions with La Revue Éclair and with other theatre companies (Théâtre à Grande Vitesse, Mandrake). She also regularly collaborates with visual artist Nicolas Cesbron. Sandrine is a specialist of body mind centering.

## HAYLEY CARMICHAEL
### Actor

Hayley Carmichael is a British actress and theatre director whose work spans TV, film and theatre. She most recently appeared in The BBC drama *Our Zoo* and is the co-founder of the critically acclaimed theatre company Told By An Idiot. She won the TMA and Time Out awards in 1999 for Best Actress for her performances in *I Weep at my Piano*, *Mr Puntilla* and *The Dispute*.

Her theatre credits include *Beyond Caring* (The Yard Theatre); *Too Clever By Half* (Manchester Royal Exchange / Told By An Idiot); *Forest* (Birmingham Rep / BIT / Barbican); *Hamlet* (Young Vic); *Fragments* (Peter Brook / Bouffes du Nord); *Sweet Nothing* (Young Vic / European Tour); *The Fahrenheit Twins* (Told By An Idiot); *Bliss* (Royal Court); *Casanova* (Told By An Idiot / West Yorkshire Playhouse / Lyric Hammersmith); *The Maids* (Brighton Festival); Cymbeline (Knee High); *Theatre of Blood* (National Theatre); *I'm a Fool to Want You* (Told By An Idiot / BAC); *The New Tenant* (Young Vic); *Zumanity* (Cirque de Soleil); *Playing The Victim* (Royal Court); *The Firework Maker's Daughter* (Sheffield Crucible Theatre); *A Little Fantasy* (Told By An Idiot); *The Birds* (National Theatre); *Aladdin* (Told By An Idiot / Lyric Hammersmith); *Shoot Me in the Heart* (Told By An Idiot / Gate / BAC); *Mother Courage* (Shared Experience); *I Weep at my Piano* (Told By An Idiot); *The Dispute* (RSC / Lyric Hammersmith); *Mr Puntila and his Man Mati* (Almeida Theatre); *King Lear* (Leicester Haymarket / Young Vic); *The Street of Crocodiles* (Theatre de Complicite).

Television credits include *Our Zoo* (Big Talk Productions); *Garrow's Law* (Shed Media / BBC); *CGI Sketch Show* (BBC); *Viva Blackpool* (BBC); *Tunnel of Love* (ITV); *Little Robots* (CBBC) and *Arrivederci Millwall* (NFTS).

Film credits include *Tale of Tales*, *Phone Box*, *The Emperor's New Clothes*, *Good Boy*, *Anazapta*, *Simon Magnus* and *National Achievement Day*.

## PHIL MINTON
### Vocal Improviser

Phil played trumpet and sang with the Mike Westbrook Band in the early 60s, then in dance and rock bands in Europe for the latter part of the decade. He returned to England in 1971, rejoining Westbrook and was involved in many of his projects until the mid 1980s. For most of the last forty years, Minton has been working as an improvising singer in diverse groups, orchestras, and artistic presentations. Numerous composers have written music especially for his extended vocal techniques. He has a quartet with Veryan Weston, Roger Turner and John Butcher, and ongoing duos, trios and quartets with many other musicians. Since the 1980s, his Feral Choir, where he voice-conducts workshops and concerts for anyone who wants to sing, has performed in over twenty countries.
www.philminton.co.uk

## STÉPHANE OLRY
### Playwright and Director

Stéphane Olry is an autodidact, his writing and productions have been staged all over France (Espace Pierre Cardin, Usine Pali-Kao, Théâtre de la Bastille, Théâtre des Bouffes du Nord, Festival d'Automne, Festival d'Avignon). He is artist in residence at the Château de la Roche-Guyon and at the Théâtre de l'Aquarium / La Cartoucherie. Stéphane founded la Revue Éclair in 1987 and has been working with Corine Miret since 1998 on developing work inspired through archival research and their own detective enquiries.
www.larevueeclair.org

## NEIL BARTLETT
### Translator

Neil Bartlett is a director, author, playwright, translator and performer – probably in that order. He has made work for the Lyric Hammersmith (of which he was Artistic Director from 1994-2005), the National, The Abbey, The Bristol Old Vic, Complicite, Handspring, The Royal Court, The Royal Shakespeare Company, The Royal Vauxhall Tavern and the Brighton, Aldeburgh, Manchester and Edinburgh International Festivals. His other translations include works by Dumas, Genet, Labiche, Marivaux, Molière and Racine. His own theatre pieces include *A Vision of Love Revealed in Sleep*, *Sarrasine*, *Night After Night*, *In Extremis* and *Or You Could Kiss Me*. His novels *Ready Catch Him Should He Fall*, *Mr Clive and Mr Page*, *Skin Lane* and (most recently) *The Disappearance Boy*, and have earned him nominations for the Costa Prize, the Whitbread Award and as Stonewall Author of the Year. You can find out more about Neil and his work, and contact him, at www.neil-bartlett.com

## CORINE MIRET
### Co-Director
Corine is an actress, dancer (contemporary and baroque) and Doctor of Pharmacy. She is the co-artistic director of La Revue Éclair together with Stéphane Olry and has performed in all of La Revue Éclair's productions. As a director she has staged *Treize Semaines de Vertu* (Thirteen Weeks of Virtue) by Stéphane Olry (Festival D'Automne 2007). As a dancer she has worked with Jean-Michel Aguis, Christian Bourigault, Isabelle Cavoit, Andy Degroat, Francine Lancelot, Marie-Geneviève Massé, Béatrice Massin, François Raffinot and Ana Yepes.

## LUC JENNY
### Lighting Designer and Technical Director
Luc Jenny trained at the Ecole Supérieure d'Art Dramatique du Théâtre National de Strasbourg. His work as a lighting designer spans theatre, dance, opera, concerts and exhibitions. He recently participated in lighting the Mont St Michel and regularly works with German artist Antonia Baehr. In theatre Luc has collaborated with French directors Bernard Bloch, François Rancillac and on numerous productions with Stéphane Olry, Corine Miret and la Revue Éclair.

Theatre of Europe commissions leading theatre directors from the continent with British creatives to premiere European work for a UK audience. Our aim is to widen access to continental European theatre practise within mainstream British theatre and we are working with some of the most exciting artists across the continent and in the UK to achieve this. Each project is developed over several years of research to build long-term relationships with the UK performing arts, to facilitate a return for the directors from continental Europe with new projects in the future and to open doors to working on the continent for participating British artists. Since forming in May 2013, Theatre of Europe has put together an ambitious programme of artists from six different European countries in partnership with leading theatres across the UK.

# print room
## *at the* CORONET

'The Print Room has fast become one of the most exciting fringe venues in London…every production it programs turns into a must-see'
*The Spectator*

'London's most upmarket fringe venue'
*Time Out*

The Print Room was founded in 2010 by Artistic Director Anda Winters, in a converted printing workshop in Notting Hill. During its time in this venue, the intimate West London theatre built a reputation for producing and curating a highly acclaimed and varied programme of performance and visual arts, including theatre, dance, music, exhibitions and multidisciplinary collaborations, in a friendly and welcoming environment.

This vision and ethos has been carried forward into the Print Room's new home, Notting Hill's The Coronet, which the charity moved to in 2014 when developers took over the original Print Room building. The theatre's inaugural season in this new space saw the Coronet building house its first theatrical performance in almost a century.

Recent theatrical highlights include the UK premieres of Howard Barker's *Lot and His God* and Jon Fosse's *The Dead Dogs*, the world premieres of Robert Holman's *A Breakfast of Eels* and Peter Gill's *As Good a Time As Any*, especially commissioned translations of Fyodor Dostoyevsky's *Notes From Underground*, the major revivals of Brian Friel's *Molly Sweeney* and Will Eno's *Thom Pain (Based on Nothing)*, as well as the reimagining of modern classics such as Harold Pinter's *The Dumb Waiter,* Arthur Miller's *The Last Yankee* and the award winning production of *Uncle Vanya.* The Print Room has also presented world premieres of new contemporary dance commissions *1898, FLOW* and *IGNIS*, as well as experimental art/opera *Triptych*.

The Coronet began life as a Victorian playhouse back in 1898, and in the 1920s became a legendary cinema. The Print Room will restore the iconic venue in stages, to take the space back to its theatrical roots.

During essential renovation work over the next few years, the Print Room will continue to create work with emerging and established artists from all fields.

**For Print Room at the Coronet**

The Print Room is a privately funded charity that receives no regular public subsidy.
We are dependent on the generosity of our supporters to present our work. Thank you to all the supporters, colleagues and friends who have helped us on our journey so far. We would not be here without their kind support.

**The Print Room is generously supported by:**
**Corporate Sponsors**

Markit are match-funders and supporters of The Print Room outreach ticket scheme.

**HEADLINE:** Allen Fisher Foundation, Clive & Helena Butler, Mike Fisher, Roderick & Elizabeth Jack, Amanda Waggott

**CAPITAL:** Anon, Ben & Louisa Brown, Glenda Burkhart, Matt Cooper, John & Jennifer Crompton, Ayelet Elstein, Lara Fares, Connie Freeman, Ashish Goyal, Tom & Maarit Glocer, Julian Granville & Louisiana Lush, Debbie Hannam, Anne Herd, Posgate Charitable Trust, The Ruddick Foundation for the Arts, Alison Winter

**Bold:** John & Laura Banes, Bill Reeves & Debbie Berger, Tony & Kate Best, Bruno & Christiane Boesch, Caroline & Ian Cormack, Victoria Gray, Cecile Guillon, Isabelle Hotimsky, Martin Jacomb, Kristen Kennish, Amy Lashinsky, David Leathers, Jonathan Levy, Tony Mackintosh, Matt & Amanda McEvoy, Julia Rochester, Lois Sieff, Rita Skinner, Antony Thomlinson, Vahiria Vedet Janbon, Pamela Williams

**Special thanks to**: Aki Ando, Paolo & Aud Cuniberti, Mimi Gilligan, Louisa Lane Fox

HERE BE LIONS

STÉPHANE OLRY
translated by Neil Bartlett

# HERE BE LIONS

OBERON BOOKS
LONDON

WWW.OBERONBOOKS.COM

This translation was first published in 2015 by Oberon Books Ltd
521 Caledonian Road, London N7 9RH
Tel: +44 (0) 20 7607 3637 / Fax: +44 (0) 20 7607 3629
e-mail: info@oberonbooks.com
www.oberonbooks.com

A catalogue record for this book is available from the British
Library.

PB ISBN: 978-1-78319-907-5
E ISBN: 978-1-78319-908-2

Cover photograph by Yves Flatard, Paris

Printed, bound and converted
by CPI Group (UK) Ltd, Croydon, CR0 4YY.

Visit www.oberonbooks.com to read more about all our books
and to buy them. You will also find features, author interviews and
news of any author events, and you can sign up for e-newsletters
so that you're always first to hear about our new releases.

## Translator's Note

In the published French script of *Hic Sunt Leones* there are no indications as to who the words of the text belong to. I have not tampered with this form of presentation.

While the idea of 'character' is complex in this text – chiefly because it deals largely with attempting (and failing) to put into words the thoughts and sensations of four people who are without any ordinary means of human communication – it is worth pointing out to any first-time reader that this is actually a documentary piece. It was created following a part-time two-year residency by Stéphane Olry and dancer Sandrine Buring at the Roche-Guyon Hospital for multiply handicapped children in France. The text 'voices' eight different people – a writer, his colleague (a dancer), two of the night-staff at the Hospital, and a quartet of that institution's inmates. These four inmates are (according to Olry); 'Kelly', a teenage *Martiniquaise* (distinguished in the text by her pink tracksuit); 'Tamara', an older but still young woman of Near-Eastern origin (distinguished in the text by her dark eyes); a pugnacious young boy called Mohammed; and a fourth child who remains undescribed but whose enigmatic expression made Stephane think of the Queen of England, and who he 'voices' accordingly. These four inmates exist both as actual people, and within the dancer's mind.

I have translated certain key words by giving their English equivalents, so that in this English version the piece is not located specifically in France – for instance, castle for *chateau*, motorway for *autoroute*. If the director and actors of any future production of this translation feel strongly that the piece needs a distinctively French location, then it would be easy to change a few details and achieve the desired effect.

The blank pages which punctuate the text are intentional, and reflect shifts or gaps in the narrative of the piece as it moves from place to place or voice to voice. They are intented to give space for breath, and reflection.

The hardest parts of the text to translate were those passages which seem to describe the inside of the dancer's head. This space is pictured in the text as a bare room containing an unholy trinity of dream-symbols of her three greatest fears or obsessions – Poverty, Institutional Power and the Body. In the course of the text, this bare room is then also populated by the four children; first by Kelly, then by Tamara, then by Mohammed and finally by the Queen of England.

'Making sense' of things – the necessity of that task, and the impossibility of that task – is largely what this text is about. As a translator, I have tried to make the text clear where it *is* clear, and trusted it to be strange when it is strange. I have neither decorated nor simplified.

Neil Bartlett
Brighton/London
May 2015

You're lying in your bed.

The street falls silent; suddenly wide awake, you rise. You move to the window. In the twilight below, you can make out shapes, moving.

Black-draped forms are gliding along the walls; skillfully, they swarm up the front of your building.

They're coming for you. That silent fancy footwork of theirs is bringing them right to your bedroom door. No security gate, no entry code and no bars are going to stop them.

Hitherto, such a prospect has always filled you with terror; this time, you've decided to fight back. You duck behind a curtain, then lie in wait in its shadow – waiting for the first one to risk climbing onto your balcony. And when he does, you're going to grab him by the throat. That's right; this time, the tables are turned. You're taking the fight to the enemy.

The proof of the pudding's in this writing.

She came by the forest road.

Her car extricated itself from the tendrils of suburbia; it slid along the electric rail of a by-pass hemmed in by multi-coloured industrial units. On a plateau punctuated by high-voltage pylons, she joined the motorway, and switched to automatic. The car elbowed its way into a forest; it rolled through rows of regimented conifers.

On the brow of the hill, the trees abruptly thinned. She stopped the car.

The white cliff of the main Hospice building, the huddled houses of the village, the well-trimmed rides and thickets of the arboretum; they slowly emerged from the icy mists rising off the river.

Her car rolled down the hill to the car park.

She skirted dustily rendered walls.

She offered her eyeball to the scrutiny of a camera. A grille slid open. Silence settled itself around her shoulders like a thick felt blanket.

Introductions were made to the New Girl in the meeting room. She was offered a coffee, then the Head of Services explained how she was going to fit in and how she'd be slotted into the timetable and who would be in charge of the children during her sessions. The rest of the meeting was just administration; we did it all electronically.

The New Girl had no idea at all what we were talking about. All she had to go on was the handshakes – the looks, the way each of us sat in our chairs.

At the end of the morning a technician fitted her with her electronic implant, giving her access to her PASS (Personnel Algorithm for Security and Socialisation) so that she could read all the conversations that had been had regarding her arrival. All the basic Hospice paperwork got downloaded for her too.

At lunchbreak, in the cafeteria, she sat right down at the end of a table, and browsed the files on her chip. While she was eating.

Oh we've been at it since the dark ages, Miss.

Over there's the quay where our predecessors used to wait for the barges to come down the river…they used to hang the babies over the side, down there by the bridge – hundreds of them, newborns, all wrapped up tight… The women would come down to the bank, look for their names written on the baby-clothes, then collect their allotted pair of brats from a bargeman. Back to the village with a kid on each tit. They had a reputation for good milk and plenty of it, the wet-nurses down here.

Then, when the Hospice was established, they got employed as wardresses.

The Hospice specialised in beggar-children, then. The regulations were all written down;

*The Dormitories shall be unheated.*
*The Children shall diet on black bread and plain water.*
*Male Children shall irrigate the Vegetables of the Home Garden and prune the Trees in the Arboretum.*
*Female Children shall weave cloth for their Uniforms.*
*All shirts will button at the back: each Child will require the Matutinal Assistance of a Comrade to dress. Thus shall they learn that Neighbourliness and Labour are better than Charity.*

When they grew up some of the Hospice Children married locally. It's their descendants who live in the village, now.

That's why we're good with the kids here; same blood. Always tell at a glance whether a new arrival's going to make it or die in the night…

Head Office always send us the trickiest cases – the ones they don't know what to do with. In the nineteenth century it was the consumptives – then, when they'd worked how to cure that, they started sending us psychotics. After proper neuroleptics became available those cases all got carted off to day care, so then we started getting the orphan ones. The more Science progresses, the more insoluble the questions the kids present – really extreme states of mind and body. Kids without any access to language, and with really reduced mobility.

You may as well get used to the fact that you'll sometimes see a crowd hanging quietly around the doors to the morgue Miss. We know what we're doing, and we always do our best, but lots of kiddies do still die here.

And you'll notice that you never see any of the children out in the village. You can hear their screams sometimes, coming through the walls, but we do like to keep them out of sight. Back in the nineteenth century Society ladies used to come down here by train to gawp at the most spectacular cases – the hermaphrodites, the skin-and-bone kids, the giants – but all that stopped years ago. We respect our kids, nowadays. Every child is individually tracked, and there's really as many categorisations and care-plans as there are cases. Every child has its own space, its own regime – its own world, really – and its own dedicated carers. Everyone sleeps in their own individual bedroom. They all have implants, so we can constantly monitor their condition. So if there's a crisis, we see it coming.

We watch them a lot. Try to understand them. But you have to not let your imagination run away with you, Miss – you can end up putting ideas into their heads that really only exist in your own. Unconsciously, I mean.

Or not.

And you have to be careful not to expect too much, too. Once you admit you're working with a lot of vegetables, well they can't let you down, can they?

Working in the Hospice is never easy. Summer holidays, some of the carers' boys and girls get taken on as casuals – and you see them going home in tears every night. I'm sure their parents do warn them what a rotten job it can be, feeding the kids – dinnertime's strictly an hour, and that's your lot – but still... You have to keep up a steady rhythm, mealtimes, and of course when a kid sicks up through its nose you've got no way of knowing whether that's the food disagreeing with them or whether they're just messed up with their plumbing somewhere...

You can have trouble sleeping.

Working in the Hospice…well, you'll see. It's heavy duty, it's full time, and it's lonely. It's like… It's like a long long silence.

Central Office send us people like you Miss because they think your sort's know-how might help. Well, it's our job to make you welcome. You never know. Perhaps somebody with a fresh pair of eyes will find a way in that we've never spotted. Good luck with that, Miss.

They admitted the New Girl to the Unit that afternoon. They'd dressed one of the kids up in her pink sweatsuit, and the New Girl took charge of her. She stayed alone with her in Psychometrics for a whole hour.

Bedded in darkness.

In silence.

Feeling nothing…; feeling… Nothing.

Nothingmovinganywhere. All immobile; lumpy. Submerged. Drowned…in myself.

Reducing myself. Boiling myself down. Concentrating myself… to a point. A small, black, distilled *point*.

Door open …fracas, lights on – *oh what a beautiful morning, you're live on air caller, porridge again, you've got a visitor this morning.* Shower; hot, cold; rustle, buttons; sharp chair corners. Tohu-bohu in the orifices. Labia of that distilled point distending, opening. Ingurgitation. Involuntary peristalsis. Digestion.

Silence. Darkness. Door closed. Smell of soap. Breakfast taste still there…

Going back into myself. Retreating. Re-grouping. Reforming. Breathing myself in. Swallowing myself whole.

Footsteps. Door open. New smell. A New Girl… Pushed – wheeled – doors swinging suddenly; empty room. Stretched muscles of the New Girl. Carried – laid – laid out on the cushioned plastic flooring…

Murmurations; ditties. Cradling. The New Girl right up close. Wrapping right round. Curled up. Huddled. Balled. Breath, voice of the New Girl. *Relax. Let me.* Night-time flesh starting to quiver. Tickling. Chuckling. The New Girl's hand. Letting her gestures invade. This one retracts; this dilates; this loosens; this one's lovely, this one pulls out. This one makes explode. Erupt. Flow.

Lava!!

Breath in; breath out. Laughing like a drain. Like a drain.

Sounding out the New Girl. Down her stiff neck. Her spine.
Entering her insides.

An empty room. A bare floor.
A cute guy, starkbollocknaked;
A dog, mangy;
An empty vessel…
Medusa!
Writhing immemorial…all-seeing tentacles…

Miss Medusa, you love to play by rules;
We love it when they're bent.
You love it when it's stiff;
We love it when things flounder.
You love it when it's up;
We love to bring things down.

You never were good with faces. In theatre foyers, they're all a blur. You smile, you pretend to recognise people, but then you turn to whoever is accompanying you and mutter *Who was that man I was just talking to?* You try and identify them by something distinctive they're wearing – a signet ring; a pair of red glasses; a khaki puffa-jacket – but then if they put the jacket in the cloakroom you introduce yourself to them all over again in the second interval. Those who know you often complain about this not being recognised; they have the definite feeling of not being invited to be part of your memories – the feeling that if they were to loiter an usher would appear from nowhere and steer them discretely towards their exit.

Nothing sticks in your brain unless you write it down.

If you don't make notes, it all just evaporates.

So you keep track of your dreams; you keep a log of all your meetings. You transcribe every single conversation.

By writing them down, you're trying to give your feelings concrete form.

To put faces to people.

To make some kind of sense of what you've seen and heard here.

They're sitting at a table with some plastic cups on it; some sachets of Nescafé; an electric kettle, a book and a pair of glasses. There are two of them.

The only light is coming from the surveillance screens – they're keeping an eye on the read-outs from the kids.

My colleague and I, we have this same discussion every single night. And we don't use the PASS to share, like we're supposed to; no, we actually have a conversation. Out loud. We find it works better.

The New Girl, the one who's working in the Psychomotricity Unit, she doesn't really talk to the day shifts. But nights, she rings the bell, we buzz her in through the glass doors, she comes up here and she has a good listen.

My colleague kicks it off;
'So, when on December the twenty-fourth
You do those little parcels,
Using the toys doled out by
Hospice Head Office;
And when that evening you deposit your packages
In front of kids
Who can neither pick them up
Nor open them,
Who gets the kick out of that?
The kids?
What do you want them to do
With your play-station consoles?
They can't even tell
A rag doll from a cuddly toy
But you, calm as you like,
You plonk your presents down in front of
Children
Who've got nothing in their skulls but air
Children
Whose limbs should have been left in the box
Who're all of a pickle
Children
Whose assembly booklet's got lost in the post

27

Never mind the operating instructions -
You're telling them what, exactly,
When you do that?'

HE:
'I'm telling them I think of them as children.'

SHE:
'No;
Like everyone else here,
You're lying to them.
If they were like other kids
D'you think their parents
Would have sent them here in the first place?'

Well you can't answer that one, can you. So you shut up.
Listen to the night-birds in the Arboretum.

SHE:
'You're saying that as far as the kids are concerned you're a god.'

HE:
'I'm saying that the kid's universe
Is what we make it.
You want to know what it's like for them?
Listen to them.
They're asleep;
They're dreaming.
That's their world, to them.
When they're asleep
They're at home.
They're happy.'

SHE:
'How can you possibly know what makes them happy?'

HE:
'They're breathing regularly –
The screens aren't indicating any fever,
Any sweats,
Or any cramps;
They're not crying;
They're not whimpering.'

SHE:
'And what can you possibly know of their unhappiness?'

HE:
'I put myself in their place.
Strangers coming and going –
Never asking if anyone minds –
Strangers who stick them with needles
Extracting
Injecting –
They're helpless.
Passive.
They can't choose anything.
They can't understand anything.
They think the universe stops
At that wall
And we drag them through it to the other side.
The ground gives way beneath them.
They tumble.
We decide everything for them.
Their world is us,
Who make it.
We're their gods,
And it's our job to protect them.'

SHE:
'Oh grow up. You really think gods protects people?'

Rest your eyes on me; I like to feel your eyes all on me. Me always in the middle, and round me, your looking; me always …held; your eyes keeping me up – black eyes, brown eyes, all kinds of eyes…tiny veins, pulsing away; some lashes that are almost white. Lids open, blink, flutter – gazes slide; gazes return. Some stares are stony; some …glance…; they balance. They never let me fall.

Open your eyes wide. I roll out my arm, letting my hand go wander over your face, stroke your sockets…fingers getting thinner…finer…invisible…till they can slide right in… I love to get *behind* when it comes to eyes, love it – stop, that's far enough, no pushing, get that thing out – I hear and obey, I'm pulling back, I'm having a sulk now…

A New Girl comes into the Unit, your looks let me drop; some rest on her hair. Some press on down to her thighs. Explore up her blouse, inspect her earrings, print off her profile…

Latch
  Shy (right up to the ceiling)
   Stroke
    Dismiss
     Enfold
      Fix
       Dash away and hide…

All alone in a pure white room…
All alone on a bright blue floor
With The New Girl.

And you – Miss New Girl – *your* eyes are grey. I reach my arm towards your face, you don't flinch, you let me…palpate…you never tell me to *Back off!!* I get right in behind the verdigris, worm my way between the bone walls and your brain, insinuate myself between the two soft pink lobes, climb some shadowy stairs, glimpse a ray of light, slip in under your door.

Into a white room;

A white room with a Medusa in a specimen jar; a girl in a pink tracksuit sprawled across the floor asleep; a white body up against a window; a black dog. The Medusa pulses in its jar. The girl in pink opens one eye. The body turns towards me. The dog's eyes lock onto mine.

HE:
'In the mornings,
It's me who opens the windows
In the units.
I tell them
Lovely day!
Bit fresher…
Snowing –
Rain or shine – snow –
Doesn't mean a thing
To the kids.
But I tell them all the same
What it's like, outside …
In the mornings.
I do their tranquilizers.
I make sure every day's
Just like the last one
And the next.
I check
That every morning
When they reach out their hands
They'll find their favourite toy
Just where it always is.
The children don't love me because I'm me
Or for what I do
But because I'm always there.
I organise their lives
So that they become *ordinary* –
No catastrophes
No to-do.
Not too much love,
Not too much hate.
No distress.
No discomfort.
An *orderly existence.*
Just like I was shown,
I endeavour to satisfy

*THE FOURTEEN NEEDS OF THE CHILDREN:*
*TO BREATHE*
*TO EAT AND DRINK*
*TO EVACUATE;*
*TO MAINTAIN AN ADEQUATE POSTURE*
*TO SLEEP*
*TO BE WARM IN WINTER, TO BE COOL IN SUMMER*
*TO BE CLEAN*
*TO AVOID ALL DANGERS…'*

SHE:
'… *TO COMMUNICATE*
*TO ACT ON THEIR OWN IMPULSES*
*TO BE FULFILLED*
*TO BE STIMULATED*
*TO LEARN*

And how's it going with those last five d'you reckon?'

HE:
'Fine.
I provide them with a simple –
An easy, an ordinary – life.
A life we can all share.
That's pretty good for starters, wouldn't you say?'

SHE:
'I don't know.
Sometimes I tell myself that for the kids
We're devils
And the Hospice, Hell.
The longer we keep them alive
The longer their sentences.
We stick feeding tubes in their stomachs.
We fuse their vertebrae so their spines can't twist.
But the kids, if they had a choice
You really think they'd ask for all this –
The force-feeding, the joint-fusing, the spinal corsets, the wheelchairs,
The thermo-formed mattresses.
The Hospice.
The daily *"And how are we this morning my lovelies?"'*

HE:

'So what d'you propose?

Hear them grinding their teeth all night and do nothing for them?

Let them choke, dinnertimes?

Leave them huddled up on their own all day?

*Close* the Hospice?

Or maybe it's me should close – shut up shop and go quietly.

Delete the memory on my sign-in card,

Dig my implant

Out of my shoulder,

And take early retirement…

Easy. But I'd still dream about them

Wouldn't I?'

You're no good with people you don't know – those faceless, elusive entities… So you use an alter-ego, a tentacle thrown out to grope its way into your chosen brave new world. You keep yourself in reserve, and the alter-ego deals with the world on your behalf.

You first took yourself off to the Hospice in March 2008. You went by car. You turned off the ring-road. You got onto the motorway. You crept under the rendered walls. The carers greeted you.

You came with a dancer. She'd come to give a class to the children.

You heard the children's cries coming down the corridors.

They opened the door to one of the Care Units for you. You went in. You saw the children for the first time. The wheelchairs. The feeding drips. The restraints and supports. The Dancer – she told you this later – took no notice of these trappings; she saw only bodies. What did she see? *Naked* bodies? The play of muscles under skin – bones, shifting subtly. To her the bodies were eloquent, but for you, they were silent.

You had nightmares every night after that.

And then, you put your back out.

Afterwards every single one of the carers told you privately that they'd also had some kind of psychosomatic response after their first encounter with the children – but the Dancer, she sailed through it. Untouched.

SHE:
'For the past ten years
It's been a rule that carers
Only ever share information via the Hospice internet –
Everything non-verbal
And all formatted according to the PASS.
All very *professional.*

The two of us only talk out loud
Because we are on night-duty.
And we only talk in front of the New Girl
Because she is, well, new.

You talk to the kids out loud too –
Like you would with a baby.
You explain everything you're doing for them –
As if that would keep them quiet…

The chat – I wonder whether it's really
To keep you calm
Or them –
I mean they always know exactly what you're going to do to them
Because, as you always say,
It's the same thing every day.
But we're not so much protecting the kids
As protecting ourselves. Aren't we?
Well – you have to fill the silence somehow.
You don't want to hear
Their loneliness.
You don't want to see
How fucked-up their lives are really,
And us just making the misery worse.'

HE:
'So why don't you resign?'

SHE:
'Everybody has to earn a living.'

HE:
'Same old answer.
Remember when you were working at Head Office
Every morning

The Tube;
The herd,
The after-shaves –
In the tunnel, when you changed trains,
The same tired old chit-chat
From the same tired old people
Heading for the same tired old desks.'

SHE:
'One morning, in a corridor,
I thought I was going to throw up.
Don't know why…'

HE:
'You asked to be transferred.
And this is where you got posted.'

SHE:
'Why are you bringing this all up
In front of Miss New?'

HE:
'So she knows no-one ends up working here by accident.'

SHE:
'That's what you think.'

HE:
'You've been here ten years;
Ten years, watching the kids sleep;
Ten years wondering whether they're trying to tell you
something in the dark –
And every night, you've come to see me.
Every night, we have the same discussion –
We know it off by bloody heart.
The questions you ask about the kids,
You're really asking about yourself.
You're only asking yourself whether their lives are worth saving
Because you've actually spent the last ten years asking yourself
What your life is worth
To you.'

And so on, every night. When they get tired of talking, one of them gets up and puts the kettle on again.

You stayed at the Hospice for several weeks.

In the evenings the Dancer and yourself used to hang out with the night-teams, and in the mornings you'd do interviews with the carers about their work.

In the afternoons, in a big empty room whose floor was covered in blue exercise mats, you'd watch the Dancer doing class with one of the children.

A teenager in a pink tracksuit.

A big lanky girl with black eyes.

You filmed the children with a video camera. *Somebody* upstairs said they were worried that you watching the children naked – with your naked eye, I mean – would make the carers see you as a voyeur. You know – invasive. Negative. And so a little *prosthesis* was suggested. You pointed out that with their contraption strapped in front of your eyes you were guaranteed not to be able to really see anything at all – that sometimes, the work has to take precedence – and politely laid the camera aside.

Watching two tangling bodies turn into a single monster, you let your mind wander wherever it wanted. Drift off …into boredom– because often the sessions seemed to give you nothing at all. Drift, until it emptied. It felt like that moment before sleep, when your limbs start to slacken across your mattress and the pictures start to crawl out of the dark…

You let yourself be taken by what you were watching like a leaf is whirled by the wind.

Oh Earth!

Still, all round me. Icy. Empty. Muscles heavy.

Oh Earth I'm afraid of letting you go. Afraid to fall. Falltumble. Without landing ever. Into the dark. Into nothing.

I tighten my tendons; grip. Batten. Spread. *Cling…* Heat spreads. Gives me a warm-up. There, inside – a throb. A pulse. Builds. Blows!!!! Strong one. Lovely. Feel the aftershocks. Shakings-up, holdings-on, lettings-go. Twisting. Sh-sh-sh-shrieking… *Possessed* – their word. *Epileptic* – their word.

Oh, Earth; quake – heave – ripple right through me…

Ah! Terror! Faultline – rips. Slices his flesh between my flesh and your flesh. Horror! Gets between us. Drags me off you. Tears me off, tears me away, drags me. Carries me.

Oh Tempest! I'm locked round your neck. You're carrying me. Your body's supple. Your skin's thin. Waist, warm. You lift me off the Earth. Bring me back to myself. Take me out of myself. I float. I fly. It's lovely.

O, Air – who are you, stranger!

Clouds part. Fog lifts – for me.

Inside, I see two children. One of them has black eyes. She's dancing with someone completely naked. The other one, the one in pink, just watches them and chuckles. A mad dog dribbles in its corner. A Medusa writhes. It's all good.

'Misery is when you're separated from the Earth. To be separated from the Earth, that's true misery.'

I've no idea either why I say that or how. The two girls just stare at me.

.

Watching this metamorphosis of child and dancer, you turn into a spectator in a darkened theatre. You've stopped moving entirely – given up all action, and even decision. Your thoughts flow freely, conjuring a bed for the Dancer and the child to nestle in. You cease to be embarrassed by the riches of this scenario. You lose yourself in dreams of this hybrid monster...

You can just imagine how in the Nineteenth century these Hospice children must been exhibited in circuses...

The chimaera notices every tremor of your immobile body. The minutest shift in posture. The tensing and relaxing of your muscles; your throat-clearings; your yawns. There, trapped in your spectator's seat, you remember movements you haven't thought of making in years, – powerful impulses which once formed you and which inhabit you still, 'though so deep inside, you're hardly aware of them, they're so much a part of you. You feel yourself – secretly, subtly – observed.

Overheard.

Scrutinised.

Sensed.

Somewhere inside the thick skull of the New Girl, there emerges …there introduces herself…invites herself – *enthrones* herself… One's Royal Self. One sees a room – wide open – and three children inside it.

First, a teenager in a fuschia t-shirt. Inside her mauve sweatpants, a black hole. One's Self is sucked up inside it. Me, Myself and I, hoovered. Masticated. Savoured. Relished. The black hole belches, and spits out One's person – One's True Self, In Person. One is then Enthroned On High at the Right Hand of the Violet Sweater Almighty.

One sees, also, in the bare room, on the empty floor; a Mongrel; a Cephalopod; a Just-As-Nature Intended-It …and a Virgin, Con Occuli Tenebrosi. Their doe-eye eye-lids bat upon My Serene Serene-ness, waiting in the wings. No fear. Let it come to pass. Let it happen. Let her proffered arm reel in My Majesty. Me, Myself and I shall surrender ourselves to this Miss Black Eyes…

A third kid lurks. Compact, rocky – Duke, Czar, Caesar. He flexes his biceps at One's Integrity. He extracts My Royal Highness-ness and inserts it in the pituitary gland of the New Girl. Enthroned, my mongrel my footstool and my gorgon my sceptre, I decree; not My Excellence alone shall rule here. Queen For a Day, Principesss Sympatica, Prima Donna Inter Pares, I gather my three little ones; we become quadrivirate. United, we declare our four wills unto our Ballerina Assoluta –

The Dancer is our vessel; we shall set sail in her.
The first one murmurs *The Dancer's screwing up her eyes.*
The second one sighs *The Dancer is wiggling one toe.*
The third, sussurrates *The Dancer rises.*
All four suggest *The Dancer should walk.*

We see through her eyes.
We hear through her ears.
We feel through her skin.
We smell through her nostrils.
We taste with her lips.

The glass doors of the Hospice swing open to let her pass.

God it was good, that beer she drank out on the terrace of the café – and the smoke of that glorious first end-of-the-day fag she lit; acrid, but comforting.

Come the evening, the dancer and you share a beer on a terrace overlooking the river.

A barge stacked with cars assembled in some factory passes on its way upstream.

You hear the Dancer predicting:
'One day
They'll post the children off in space-ships
Millions of light-years away from the Earth.
They'll travel protected inside some kind of cocoon…
And when they make it to the planet they're meant to colonise
The children will split their chrysalises,
Shake out their wings
And fly like butterflies
Through a world that's finally fit to be their home.'

YOU:
'The kids don't live in outer space.
They're living our future –
A world of individuals isolated in separate cells,
Coming long distance –
Each living out a separate dream
And compensating for the poverty of the body
With a plethora of image and spectacle.'

THE DANCER:
'I'd say
People remove any possibility of getting through to the children
When they forbid themselves to touch them.
It's bodies that understand bodies.
That's how – for instance – they tell me they don't want their blood taken
Unless the needle's being handled by a nurse they like.'

YOU:
'The children speak to you?'

The dancer shrugs her shoulders.

You watch her and wonder;

'Do you really believe
In a universal language of bodies?
A Paradise lost
Just beath the skin –
Buried in the bones, the muscles, the guts?'

The dancer stands up. She drops some change on the table. You watch her walking off down the tow-path.

You say to yourself; 'Every step she takes on earth, she feels herself born up by one single great living creature.'

The New Girl was summoned to a meeting to evaluate her work at the Hospice. All the principle parties involved were present, and correct. The positive and negative aspects of her work were listed, and a conclusion was drawn.

'You did the children no harm. Possibly you did them some good. But were you of any *use?*'

The New Girl gasped. 'Being in love,' she said, 'Is that ever any *use?*'

The kids – we, the four children – are right here inside the Dancer.

There's no seating. The room we occupy is empty – its floor bare. The pariah whimpers in his sleep. The Medusa fixed us with its stare.

We feel the Dancer's body swaying like a sedan chair, ordered for our pleasure. We sense the steady beating of her heart. We heard that last conversation they had with her, and we realised how we could – we, the four children could – raise her pulse-rate and get her blood racing by joining in her games. We can already hear plasma bustling down arteries, the slow seepage through the mucous membranes, the opening and closing of sphincters.

On the surveillance screens, a close eye is being kept on the New Girl's movements. She takes the same walk every evening. She heads along the river, beside the drainage ditch.

We – the four children – suggest to the Dancer that she stop for a bit. That she close her eyes.

The croaking of a frog. The eight strokes of the Hospice chapel bell.

Sounds come at us from every direction.

A slight commotion in one of those ditches. We, the four children, whisper to the Dancer that she should lean out over the culvert to see what's happening. When she does it she disturbs a flight of the bats who were roosting just a few feet below her, and we laugh to think that by simply suggesting she might be curious about something we've triggered all that panic. The Dancer seems undisturbed by the rustling of the night-creatures.

Has she even noticed them? Is she lost in thought?

In anxious thoughts.

Thoughts of us…

The pariah wakes. With one growl, he scatters us – us, the four children.

Poverty! Most discreet of disfigurements; dirtiest of all disabilities… Yes, that's it, what's dogging me – *hounding* me – isn't Depression – it's *Poverty*. Just enough to live on, but never enough for a good time – oh a coffee at the counter with mates, fine, sure, but a restaurant, never. Always, *calculation* – the incessant whisper of bills, the clink of counted change – *useless* adding-up – addition, subtraction; Obsession. Shame. Secrecy. And an unfurnished room, with a clutter of bedclothes on the floor – 'Oh no, no mattress, it's better for my back' – and that pre-recorded voice announcing that *owing to overdue payments, service has currently been suspended.* Bitch! Slut! Scheisekopf! Alone every night with just this mangy mutt for company, waiting to be fed. Aches. Age. Humiliation. Anxiety – all the time – a millstone round my neck. Lockdown.

The only way out; the Medusa. The Institution. A cure worse than the disease…

Following the Dancer's thoughts, we – the four children – light on the specimen jar, where lurks that gelatinous creature with tentacular eyes. 'Use! Were you of any *Use?*' – Damn her, the bitch – Writhing, All-Seeing Bitch Institution … Expenses claims for every bite you eat; reports; plans; budgets. Outlines. Ten-line summaries. Proposals. All in writing…and if I write, I don't dance. If it's all there in the proposal, no need to actually make the show, huh? Oh Miss Jellyfish never answers questions. You always have to guess what she wants next. She's never happy, and she's always hungry. Result; bile, nausea, stomach cramps, ruined joints, ruined digestion, a ruptured gall-bladder, a twisted spine. Stiff neck. Fused vertebrae. *Petrifaction.*

'Miss Jellyfish turns me to jelly, Miss Jellyfish turns me to jelly…'

That's the chant that we, the four children, keep up while the Dancer tramps the weed-choked rides of the Arboretum. Using her nostrils, we scent the trees she's striding through. In just one step, the sharp and sugared fragrance of rotting windfalls gives way to the resiny essence of black pine. We relish every moment of this shop-full of odours. We encourage our hostess to gather an apple that has rolled right to her feet. We entice her into bringing the fruit close to her face. The smell of still-green apple penetrates her nostrils. We whisper to the Dancer *Bite deep.* The taste invades her, expands and is exhaled. Then, we, the four children, we invite the Dancer to repeat her crime; to crunch once again through the apple's sharp skin, to chew its flesh, release its juices, taste and then swallow – *Slowly!!!* – letting us savour the sensations for as long as possible. And all of this anatomical exertion – suggested by us, the four children – gives rise to the following thought in the Dancer's mind;

'ohwhatagreatapple.'

On the surveillance screens, New Girl is seen to be turning her steps towards the metal gates of the Arboretum. She's seen walking out of range of the last camera on the perimeter. Seen taking the path towards the cliffs by the river.

We, the four children, we feel every footstep she plants on those pebbles, feel it lift from the soil, fight free of gravity, then return to earth on the path. The regular pace she keeps up as she carries us through the forest increases our pleasure, step by step by step.

Up in the empty room, the naked body comes up to us, takes us by the hand and begins to lead us in a gentle round.

The old dream…of having a tail growing out of my spine. A tail to balance me in every step, every *arabesque*. A great big bushy tail I could roll myself up in to sleep… One day, my body broke. It slammed the door on me – said it had had had enough of my whining and laid me out on the parquet. So there I was; staring at the ceiling. Couldn't even lift my little finger. Barely blink. Spent whole days on that parquet, while my body went its own sweet way, free at last. And then…finally…it came back. Made it up with me again. Was tamed. By babbling, I re-learnt its language.

So why, after all that, endure the yapping cur? Why, the diktats of the Medusa?

For my body. So that through my body I can meet other bodies, like the bodies of those children

The Dancer and us – us the four children – we're sinking into darkness now. There we are up on the hill; we've crept back out to watch the lamplighters light up the Hospice car park.

To follow the silver ribbon of the river down below.

To just make out the great dark mass of the forest.

Safe behind your curtain, you watch the intruders scramble up onto your balcony. But you don't grab them by their throats. You don't grab them by the hoods of their jackets. You let them come right up to you. You know exactly what they want.

In the silence of the Psychomotricity Unit, you give yourself over to the seductive spectacle conjured up by that chimaera. You watch the spittle dripping. The fluids leaking. You listen to the laughs, the gurglings, the coughs, the gasping, rasping breath – heavy, sometimes; sometimes, held – the skins sliding over each other, stroking each other; the fibres of the muscles stretching and retracting. You can see how much trouble and how much joy there is in these exchanges between Child and Dancer. Some part of what they are sharing seems always to reveal itself to you somehow. Do you feel at all frustrated? Of course you do.

You'll be able to supply what's missing with your imagination. What you don't know, you'll write.

Like those ancient Latin-speaking map-makers, you won't just leave a blank where people tell you there's a desert or some as-yet-undiscovered country. You'll fill in the blank with writing:

*Hic sunt leones.*

Here, be lions.

www.ingramcontent.com/pod-product-compliance
Ingram Content Group UK Ltd.
Pitfield, Milton Keynes, MK11 3LW, UK
UKHW031250020325
455689UK00008B/116